Balkan Poetry Today
2018

Balkan Poetry Today

2018

Editor:
TOM PHILLIPS

red hand
BOOKS

First published in 2018 by **Red Hand Books**
Kemp House, 152-160 City Road, London
EC1V 2NX

www.redhandbooks.co.uk

This compilation copyright © 2018
All rights in the works printed here revert to the authors,
translators and original copyright holders after publication

Balkan Poetry Today is published annually by
Red Hand Books, England

This edition: 978 1 910346 25 9

A CIP catalogue record for this book is
available from the British Library

Prepared for publication by red hand books
Cover design © red hand books

Contents

II POETRY

With especial thanks to all the translators: Oana Andreea Axon; Fadil Bajraj; Tanja Bakić; Cristina Berinde; Alistair Ian Blyth; Jasmina Bolfek-Radovani Mina Ray; Peter Constantine; Sean Cotter; Mircea Dan Duta; Karen Emmerich; Vlad Alui Gheorghe; Genta Hodo; Leni Idrizi; Cristina Ilie; Danijela Jovanović; Marija Krivokapić; Florina Luminos; Stephen J. Mangan; Natasha Miladinovic; Milena Milkova; Alexander Mitovski; Shqiptar Oseku; Ivana Pantelić; Svetlana Pavlović; Tatiana Purice; Angela Rodel; Anca Roncea; Ralitsa Saramova; Olimpia Sârb; Alina Savin; Claudia Serea; Adam J. Sorkin; Peter Stonelake; Danijela Trajković; Galina Tudyk; Lidia Vianu; and those poets who translated themselves.

Tom Phillips is a poet, playwright and translator now living in Sofia, Bulgaria. His poetry has been published in numerous journals and anthologies, as well as in the full-length collections *Unknown Translations* (Scalino, 2016), *Recreation Ground* (Two Rivers Press, 2012) and *Burning Omaha* (Firewater, 2003). It also features on *Colourful Star*, the online art/poetry project he runs with the artist Marina Shiderova, and has been translated into Albanian, Bulgarian, Italian, Macedonian, Romanian, Serbian and Spanish. Tom has participated in a number of international literary festivals, including World Poetry Day in Romania, the Aca Karamanov poetry weekend in Macedonia and Sofia Poetics, as well as an Sofia's Poetry on the Metro project. A former translator-in-residence at the Sofia Literature and Translation House, he has translated work by many of Bulgaria's leading contemporary poets. Tom's other work includes the plays *No Time For Hope* (Bristol, 2017), *Coastal Defences* (Bristol, 2014) and *100 Miles North of Timbuktu* (Bristol, 2013), as well as essays and travel writing about SE Europe.

Editorial

Welcome to *Balkan Poetry Today 2018* – the second issue of the annual journal dedicated to contemporary poetry from SE Europe. Following the extremely positive reaction to 2017's edition, we are delighted to be publishing another extraordinarily diverse and engaging selection of new translations of more than forty poets and we hope that you will enjoy reading work which encompasses everything from the lyrical and reflective to the philosophical and conceptual.

As with the previous issue, we have included two sections focusing on specific countries – in this case Romania and Moldova. These are almost entirely the work of Mircea Dan Duta – whose own poetry featured in *Balkan Poetry 2017* – and I am extremely grateful to him for the huge efforts he has gone to in order to gather, collate and, in many cases, translate the work of so many strong and individual voices from those two countries as well to ensure that these sections offer a representative range of the work being produced by different generations of poets.

Mircea's support has been invaluable, as has that of two other stalwart contributors: Danijela Trajković, who sourced the selection of Serbian poetry included here, and Adil Olluri, who did the same for the Albanian-language work in this issue. I would also like to thank Jasmina Bolfek-Radovani for allowing us to print her fascinating essay on writing multilingual poetry and for her help with Croatian poetry. Many of the contributors to *BPT17* have also done much to support the project, promoting the journal and identifying other poets we might publish. Above all, though, I want to thank Richard and Carole Eccles at Red Hand Books, whose ongoing commitment remains absolutely crucial and without whom there simply wouldn't be a *Balkan Poetry Today*. My name may well appear on the cover as editor, but this is a collaborative project. I'm sure that this is one of the things which has contributed to its distinctive 'atmosphere' and which, for me, makes it a particularly exciting publication to work on.

Tom Phillips
Sofia, Bulgaria

I POETRY FROM ROMANIA

Magda Cârneci

An immense hand

The fire-glory of the morning.
I advance blind through the dense light. solid.
I stagger. it's not permitted for me to stagger.
I bear within me something more ferocious than dynamite.
more corrosive than nothingness.
the tumoral dawn rose of the world. its petals
slowly unfurl in my brain, carbonized
like a self-contemplating planet. in flames, all in flames.
I feel its acrid smell of child and corpse.
it's ready to bloom. I hear its heavy respiration.
slowly it unfurls in my brain, the rose
of millions of petals. drops of sweat
and silent blood drip down
      it's making ready to come down

     to come down   to come down

        an immense hand holds me in its palm.

Translated by Adam J. Sorkin

Wheel, ruby and vortex

wheel, ruby and whirl,
  the luminous snow of your lips guided me through the garden
there where I saw no woman, no man
  only the gleam of the twilight dawn,
swallowed in the end by your never-ending sweetness
  a mist among leaves
there, where in the end there's nobody
  only an infinite fragrance
and fingers left behind on the shore

will this world be raised on wings?

Translated by Adam J. Sorkin

Poetical paradise

in the library's concentric studio, the coral tree glowed white with flowers
in the palace of a thousand rooms near the scribe's vestibule
a green labyrinth was budding like a pristine eyeball
there one sees the reflection of a polished malachite terrace
of a round-and-square town carved in a pearl
immersed in the roar of a celestial river
flowing whole as a single drop in an opened book, in which
only the perfect man's exaltation can read anything.

Translated by Adam J. Sorkin

Caius Dobrescu

Marius the Karpathian
Fragment from the 23rd chapter of the verse novel Euromorphotikon

...But one night, who knows
what magical filters they poured in the champagne, and we've
    seen ourselves sliding suddenly into their
arms. We let them feel us all over, caress us, flood
    our faces with their viscous Vital Fluids. Suck us until
we became carcasses. Then they pulled us to their Land Rover and
    away we went. And when we woke up... Well,
we were already on the Island of Aragnon. With no idea
    of the Event or the Common Declaration, but we
liked the premises and the fact that, at the ID control, when they
    saw we were Karpathians, they showed us immediately to
what is called the Eastern Auxiliary Think Tank, so that
    the disgusting Antônho and Leonorh had to remain behind
the barbed wire. Actually we did not
    feel outraged by this discrimination. Simona and I
did not intend anyhow to take part in the East-European
    Mini-Congress of the Abundant Love, which, we heard rumours, had to
reach its own separate agreement, to be included
    at a later date in the Common Declaration...Bla-bla... We had
nothing to do with this. We were happy to rest
    and breathe the fresh breeze... But truth be told,
DCI Shaftesbury, our joy was but short-lived. It is not only
    that we were not totally delivered from Antônho
and Leonorh, since in the time destined to common usage
    of the Central Beach we still had to
observe the contract by which they bought our souls, but neither
    could we preserve our intimacy when we managed to
cut lose from our cruel oppressors. I was too
    sick of my- and she of herself. We couldn't
find even the power to embrace, not anymore. And to
    crown it all, DCI Shaftesbury, in this so-called
Think Tank we discovered a kind of hell much worse
    than what we experienced with Antônho
and Leonorh. Actually we were in
    a hornet nest. Ripe with intestine wars
and horny sticks poured from all sides on us.

Translated by the author

4

Dinu Flamand

The empress' carpet
Vienna, December, 2015

I had gone to greet Brueghel and maybe even
to scrounge something from the wooden stretcher
that two country bumpkins
carry running through the luxurious Viennese museum
as if they were out
yobs of the Flemish painting with the rural wedding
and already wobbling drunk

...but I got confused regarding the sense of a visit
and bumped into Maria Theresa
mournfully reigning in that
pietas austriaca
namely that doing her best under her layers of
black lace to look sad
after the death of her former under-husband
and former under-emperor of that
Holy Germanic and former Latin Empire
with annexes through Transylvania and
later even in Bucovina.

And in the composition of the imperial desolation
a single colour patch could afford
the painter of the court – indicating that only the symbol
of that beloved garden could still ease
the bitterness of this Grandmother of Europe
(I copy explanations out of the catalogue).

What is this that I see:
she was stepping right on
MY
Transylvania
that had become a carpet-province
trampled with a bovine grandeur.

How the hell to tell her to move her feet
from there?
She ruined my day.

Translated by Olimpia Sârb

5

El excremento del Dios
Ciudad de Mexico, November 17, 2017

It was called *El excremento del Dios* if made
from *nauhatl*
in the language of the conquerors
we can trust this translation.

Take into consideration that not the mystical humiliation
but the pride itself
to be the result of a divine combustion
or fertilizer for the future
must have been the substance of that name.
Otherwise, it was called *Cuitláhuac*
and he was a brother to Moctezuma
the Emperor killed with all sorts of cunning
by Cortés;
he had become the penultimate warrior chief
but the first Aztec rebellious
who no longer feared, neither the horses,
neither the armour, neither the harquebuses,
nor the cross of the strutting Hispanics.

He had assembled half a million warriors
and even if barefoot his were about ten times
more numerous than the footwear-wearing Hispanics,
and their wood bludgeons encrusted
with obsidian
chips and the lances and arrows and
the black daggers
sculpted out of volcano spit
would have turned the civilizing ones into slivers.

If the pox had not resisted them –
it would have meant an unknown
excrement of destiny for them.

And when destiny suffers from looseness of the bowels
the last emperor of the losers
Cuauhtémoc
himself couldn't bear another name
than *The Descending Eagle*.

Translated by Olimpia Sârb

Iulia Militaru

The definition of a term necessary to the post-demonstration: the fugue

Through fugue, or run, we usually understand:
Either *moving with big, fast steps,*
or *leaving a place in a hurry*
    to escape a constraint or a danger.
There is also the exceptional meaning: the fugue,
Polyphonic musical form with two or more voices,
    in which the melody played by one voice is repeated in turn
    and developed by the other voices according to the counterpoint laws.
And also the unusual meaning: the fugue and the death,
a case of partial synonimity between two
simple common nouns of feminine gender.

For poetry and its readers,
however free they think they are,
only the unusual and the exceptional meanings
    will always matter.
Everything else disappears in the amorphous mass
    of usual presences
    and ordinary catachreses.

Translated by Claudia Serea

The fugue and the death

The fugue and the death   two words
different meanings   common language

Demise,
liberating stimulations of the matter.

Crying,
hypertrophiated lacrimal glands.

This is how things should go,
nothing abnormal, nothing strange.

*

And yet,
Dacians were laughing at funerals,
nothing abnormal, nothing strange.
Laughter stimulates endogenous endorphins
and reduces the risk of cancer.

But paradox follows the human being.

Death caused by too much laughter is both a particular and exceptional
situation. Usually, it occurs through cardio-respiratory stoppage.
From antiquity to the present day, many cases of killer laughter have
been recorded. More information here: http://filosofiatis.blogspot.
ro/2014/12/ars-moriendi.html

Physiopathology: Numerous problems of human anatomy and
physiology transform benign laughter into a ferocious killer. Thus,
lesions of the brain stem, of the bridge of Varolio and of the medulla
can trigger pathological laughter, causing atony and syncope, followed
by other lesions, such as those of the hypothalamus. These can extend
to the cerebellum.

Epode: Emotional lability is just a simple sign of the predisposition to
death by laughter/never a cause of it.

Dying (of laughter) is no joke!

Translated by Claudia Serea

Is there a death law?

All of these signs were recently graded.
No one ever believed there is a death law,
(let alone, a definition of it; only images)
One could die and live as they pleased:

1. Suicide by firearm, September 20, 1890, female; the following note was found: *Beloved Vasile, if you'd like to do me a last favour, please pay the washerwoman 7 lei and 50 bani; I wouldn't want her to curse my soul; and to the kerosene seller I have to pay 1 leu and 75 bani; if you want, ask the French woman or the maid to pay him. Please don't deny me my last wish. And one more thing. Please, I'm asking you, when I'm dead, show some interest in me, do something, anything you want, to show you're sorry, or do what you know, but do it so the world can see. You know very well this is not for me, because I won't know anything; but for you, because there are some people who know my entanglement and they will gossip a lot behind your back. They are already, even without this. Please, listen to me, do something to save your reputation, something that wouldn't cost you money you don't have. Please listen, I know what I'm saying. Forgive me for giving you advice, it's because I don't want you to have any troubles because of me. Kisses!*

2. Suicide by poisoning with phenic acid, November 21, 1890, male; the following note was found: *Look, I'm drinking phenic acid; I'm poisoning myself!*

3. Suicide by poisoning with arsenic, December 11, 1898, unspecified sex; no note was found; in the morgue archive's log, one can read: *He didn't say he was sick with anything; but for a while this person was very sad.*

More abuse occurred.
Denying death, overvaluing life,
the absence of a clear explanation for
being alive.

Lastly, the ultimate confusion.

Epode: They resorted to SCIENTIFIC/research.

Translated by Claudia Serea

Ioan Es. Pop

beyond

it's been nearly thirty years since beyond went away. a little before and then during my time, beyond was the only place that really existed, the only place worth living for. beyond was food and drink to us, hearth and home. incredible things were said about it. it worked inside us with terrible power. it made possible the day still to come, although that day was the same as yesterday, the same as tomorrow.

vienna, budapest, belgrade... everything came from beyond and everything happened beyond. when nothing seemed possible any longer, beyond was the only possible thing, although no one had ever actually run across it. love lived beyond. fortune lived beyond. hope lived beyond. god lived beyond.

then suddenly beyond was right here. but when we reached beyond, we found out it was not what we had been dreaming of. ten years later, when no more was said about beyond, we in fact understood the farther we advanced beyond, the farther away beyond became. it was no longer in vienna, neither in budapest nor belgrade, not even in london or paris.

now i know: if we keep on longing for it with all our might, we will have to go beyond beyond, so far beyond that no trace of here would be left. could we reach it by train? never. by ocean liner? no, no matter how many seas we crossed. by airplane? not even if we travelled a thousand years without a stopover. in its own unique way, however, beyond seems somewhere near us, very near. it just doesn't move in our direction.

Translated by Adam J. Sorkin and Lidia Vianu

october 12, 1992

i've returned home after long years of
wandering around bucharest
i've returned with an empty string bag in my hand.
she comes to the gate and says, well,
my dearest, you promised you'd make money.
you said that in two years you'd earn more than others earn in four,
and look, you're bringing back nothing.

listen to me, my dears, i earned nothing.
i'm bringing home more nothing than anyone could
have saved in these two years.
i've hardly been able by myself to carry
all the nothing i've earned.

behind me come carts heaped high with nothing,
near to breaking under the weight.
when all are unloaded in our yard,
nobody will have as much nothing as we.

in a year or two it will be more valuable than gold.
we'll sell it after when the price goes sky-high.
my dears, rest assured, nobody has as much nothing.
i've saved it for two years, thinking only of you.

Translated by Adam J. Sorkin and Lidia Vianu

when i was a small child, i dreamt of being even smaller

smaller than the table, smaller than the chair,
smaller than my father's big boots.
no bigger than a potato is how i dreamt of myself.
because in spring they put po-
tatoes in the ground, and that's it,
they never bother about them till autumn.

i dreamt of curling up in a hole among them,
sleeping sweetly in the dark,
turning to one side and the other all summer long,
then falling asleep once again.

in autumn i awaken still unrested,
unwashed like my brothers,
and when the spade thrusts near i leap out
and shout: stop digging, stop digging,
i'll gladly come back home
if in spring you return me here.

so in spring i'm the first
they drop down into the hole.
in this way i could go on sleeping forever:
from the ground to the cellar, from the cellar to the ground,
year after year, undisturbed and forgotten.

Translated by Adam J. Sorkin and Lidia Vianu

Anca Bucur

Reality – a geo-political definition

Reality designated territory, a spread, a space circumscribed or boundless, general size, non-exclusively associated with a state, however enough to ensure that which is necessary for survival, food and protection for a social group. That which escapes the inclusion in a territory and the capture in a state apparatus is the nomadic population. The nomad has no direction, trajectories or ground even though they obviously have some of everything. For if the Nomad can be named the Deterritorialized *par excellence* it is precisely because, to them, reterritorialization doesn't occur after, as it does for the migrant, neither elsewhere, as is the case of the sedentary. For the nomad, on the contrary, deterritorialization itself is his connection to the ground, so that he reterritorializes on deterritorialization itself. Because of that the nomad doesn't become subordinated, he doesn't connect or branch to a centre of power. Through counter-placement and distribution, he evades a politico-territorial demarcation and normative coordinates, but not a localization. The nomad distributes himself in a smooth rhyzomic space, he occupies, lives and controls that space and this is where his territorial principle resides. Therefore, it is not by chance that the nomad's trajectory is drawn ad continuum, nonstopping and nonlinear, broken by the polyvocality and variability of directions, by bunched relays, by the system of stations communicating, intermediating.

[to live, a being without a citadel:
midst of a steppe ash
watching from afar movements of bipeds
the swish of clothes when touched,
of brushwood thumping under
ground their steps
crossing at an insignificant distance
close to   the edge
of the sill,
the small   eyelets   in the wall
the body begins
to listen carefully around:

fact of 99 faces/ fact of 99 sorts
fact of clay, fact of man/ fact of maiden, fact of boy
snake skinned/ wolf mouthed
rabbit holed/ dust graved
fact of loss and fact of foul

13

when night is halfway passed
and young life flows out
under
weeds
morning finds you with your eyes
caught in a white coating
waiting for the call and the pack,   taming
you as leviathan among gods
beast among sovereigns
and every fold of the body
you hear them heedlessly fluttering
with the twisting offspring
on the lath fence.]

Translated by Anca Roncea

Daniel Bănulescu

Keep giving all you've got for the last hundred metres

How could you not know? You knew
You knew with every single cell
How, after an hour together in line
Sexual desire would overwhelm us
You'd turn pale I'd pant
And we'd make it only as far as the elevator

You drive me crazy
You brush your fingers over my temples and drive me crazy
As you whisper softly and open your mouth so wide
That I can see down to your intestines
Excited tense and ready
Lashing their tails
Waiting for me to take you

How could you not know? You're much more beautiful than any other
woman
More fiery more profound more tender
Than any other woman in the world
Even though you're just you
Even though your breasts are the nicknames
God gave you
Back in those days when he created flesh

And you amaze me
You call out my name get close and amaze me
In the room of your body I always sit front and centre when we watch TV

In the bedroom I have the bed
In the kitchen I have the three-legged Viennese trivet for coffee
But you turn pale
We pant
We make it only as far as the elevator

Translated by Adam J. Sorkin, Lidia Vianu, Alina Savin

It's good to be Daniel Bănulescu
At the 'Bar of my Wound'

The dog came close and sniffed me all around.
I let him taste my wound.

I let him. He tasted it. And grew even stronger.
A stray dog. A fighting dog. He grew doggier.

He came in and sprawled on the counters as if entering hell.
There inside my soul. The wine-cellars of my blood. At the 'Bar of my Wound'.

My girlfriend came close and sniffed me all around.
"You've no idea what nonsense it babbles in its sleep, your wound."

I got up and left her then and there. She became a cobweb between two coffees.
Inside my soul. At the 'Bar of My Wound'.

The devil came close and sniffed me all around.
"I'll found a Theological Institute in your wound."

I prayed till my sweat glittered like a basket of memorial candles.
Then God turned the Devil into a stuffed Devil. At the 'Bar of My Wound'.

Where the back of a hand won't knock the glasses aside.
Where nobody don't know nothing 'bout nobody's soul inside.

Where sudden pity stabs you in the back. Under the window.
Where the blackbird won't sing. Nor the wind blow.

Translated by Adam J. Sorkin, Lidia Vianu, Alina Savin

Carmen Secere

I was looking sadness in the eyes
my shadow was sweating

people are leaving you told me
and behind you the city collapsed

I was living incognito
on the last floor

Translated by Oana Andreea Axon

copper's

ripped jeans stained with whiskey
and a crumbled jazz
on blackened keyboards

the stinging smell
of cremated love

I care not giving nights away for mercy
it only hurts when others don't know how to share them

I'm dancing on the table
in the free entrance tavern
laughing
and the laughter is ripping me

Translated by Oana Andreea Axon

brown skin smelling like seaweed
the french cajun lispy accent
and magnolia's morning
in convex mirrors

your feet don't return
through the bleeding street's ashes
anymore

april is flooding us
with our underground rains
from new orleans

Translated by Oana Andreea Axon

Adrian Suciu

To drink alone

No one knows what it's like to drink so alone
that you give a name to your brandy. Many sat
at the bleak table, but what to speak
with some who do not know the name of your brandy?

No one knows what it's like to drink so alone
that you give a name to your blood. He is the only one that keeps you
company. Until one day.

No one knows what it's like to drink so alone
that you give a name to your solitude.
You should be the one to take
this dusty and tearing woman out in the city!
Someone will comfort her for sure!

No one knows what it's like to drink so alone
that even your loneliness will not stay
with you at the table...

Translated by Cristina Berinde

Lungs

Everything is about breathing.
About how you breathe in. There are
many types of air. Sometimes the air is like a bullet.
Other times it's like the lottery jackpot
won by a dying man. There are more
types of breathing than the doctors can count.

With one breath you comb your life, which is tiny,
like you would comb the hair of a late doll.
With one breath the cold blushes
and lies on the bed.
With one breath you realize that time
is a train with many wagons carrying serenity
to nowhere.

From lungs we come and to lungs we shall return.

Translated by Cristina Berinde

With substance

Write with substance! Writing with ink
it's toxic. Writing with words is churning of chaff.
Use the word! But not to make it
a carpet. Not to be delighted about how great you are
but to wonder about how little you can be.

The word is ice. Hold the floe in your arms
until it becomes litres and litres of liquor
that you will spread at the tables.

Take your bottle and walk!

Translated by Cristina Berinde

Andrei Zbîrnea

Adela's arms

this frame invaded by a virgin's hands
I designed it on an autumn morning
I sat at the table and wrote
behind the black boxes
the smell of fresh grass overwhelmed
the smell of blood of the
kamikaze lost in Baghdad
Adela's arms were amputated
by the black box of the last airbus
stranded in the north of the Atlantic
after this major event
Adela was not Adela and
her hands were given to recent

history as
a sign of solidarity.

Translated by Vlad Alui Gheorghe

tango lessons

the sky rolled over your thighs hollows you are looking at me from the
dim light you are
not wearing the red dress anyway I think it is not suitable for a rainy day
you don't really know how to dance anymore not long ago you were
teaching the autistic people
how to dance tango you sang me a requiem of a funeral march something
inside you got lit off
no more tears or smiles your face is invaded by cherry blossoms
and yet you are happy
with your new mechanics the hollows of your thighs underwent thermal
inversions you want to read something to me but I am lost in the steps of tango.

Translated by Vlad Alui Gheorghe

Peter Sragher

ode to stalin

the old poet makes
      the mandolin
sing russian songs
      on the danube
and his white hair
bears in mind
how he loved
      the russian language
his eyes wished
they danced *kalin kakalin kamaia*
but their sight is blurred now
so that he whispers to
      the other poet
with a voice from
      his youth
his poem *ode to stalin*
that once
made him immortal

2 June 2008

Translated by the author

25

with each move

to lieven

he changed the geometry
        of the place
the mound of sand sat in
        his hands
and he sat on air
with eyes closed
he was looking into
        the distance
a breeze of air touched his
        knees
and cast another shadow
        on the earth
he did not see anything
breathing in the silence
breathing out the silence
        to the sea

Costineşti & Bucharest 3 & 5 June, 31 July 2008

Originally written in English

II POETRY

Roman Kissiov

The poet can

They said:
A poet cannot feed a family

They said:
A poet can feed
Only the worms...

O, no –
The poet feeds the pigeons
The poet feeds the eagles
The poet feeds the angels
The poet feeds the hearts –
       the hearts of people
       still hungry
       for Truth and Light...

The poet can feed thousands
with but five verses

Translated by Ralitsa Saramova

Procession of the words

A long procession of words
against the whiteness of the paper.
A funeral procession...
Whom are the words burying?
The words are parting with their author.
The words are following and mourning over
the poet's life on earth –
even though he's still alive,
even though he isn't in the Land Beyond...

The poems written years ago
outlived the man bearing my name
that I was then.

Translated by Ralitsa Saramova

Obren Ristić

Afternoon in the suburb

Crying cries and hoarse music
on the radio from a nearby house

Last move of a rooster
reflection of the axe
and sprinkled apron

and nothing happened again

Translated by Danijela Trajković

Long night, very long

They've brought us down into a long night!

The homeland forests are behind us
and all the secrets.

The ancestors wrapped their heads under their arms
in the east of Serbia
in the highest nest of an eagle.

For so many summers
my father and I
have been walking around the hearth in silence
with our heads bent down
waiting for the baby eagles
to hatch.

The night of great deception
lasts for too long.
Dogs are barking,
not a single word from messengers.

Translated by Ivana Pantelić

Erenestina Gjergji Halili

To the cathedral

I have to get to the cathedral
Carrying a load, carrying a word

I have to get to the cathedral
In the hustling night, through endless dark

I have to get to the cathedral:
A man acts by his word and the word has been given,
So I have to get to the cathedral.

Soul full of peace, sky filled with my son
I have to get to the cathedral

I've bent my head, I've yielded my heart
To the given word, at the cathedral

A voice is hushing in glowing timbre
I have to get to the cathedral

The ironhead bell slowly wobbles,
The steps are hasty, at the cathedral

The wordless darkness darkens the night,
The man of word, who kept his word,
Has stopped breathing, at the cathedral...

Translated by Genta Hodo

Dimitris Athinakis

Conventional poem

My teeth grind every night as I lie in bed,
they strive to edge into place
taking time to settle
      in search of justification.

Every night my teeth go creek-creek-creek
gravediggers in cemeteries
snatching coins from the eyes of the dead.

My teeth will not stay where they are –
one by one they will come out as I grow
      and
fling themselves into the outside world,
imprisoned as they've been
within lips, spit, gums, and cheeks,
so many years in darkness
they yearn for light
– laughter, whatever you might say, was never permanent.

My teeth grind every night as I lie in bed.
However much I smile in the evenings
they know
that morning will come soon enough,
and they'll once more begin

to make believe that they are slicing up words.

Translated by Peter Constantine

So they said

You knew you were walking alone
– no rage anymore –
down a wintry road
This road, so they said, was overgrown with weeds
no rage anymore

[and you walk]

Behind you how the earth disappeared
and the trees swallowed the birds
even the sky itself

It was, so they said, the persecution
from the city you abandoned
and you were leaving, so you said, it was your turn
for it to disappear and disappear and disappear
that place where you triumphantly stepped

[you don't know where you're going]

You can't, so they said, take cover
any longer
from beautiful summers

[so they say]

It was – where are you walking? – the battle of time with need
It was – where are you walking? – the war that broke without
rest
Without anything resembling a human anywhere around

[where are you walking?]

It was with us, so they said, the desire for a trip
to another planet

[it too alone, so they say, and scared
by the howls of nature –
everyone has their own
– what did you think?]

It was a wind that broke that night
stealing the sounds of the forest and
it never gave them back

to let them feel the world
– another, greener, perhaps more lonely world

[no
no one is alone
no one is left alone
– we thought together]

The wind, though, look, it came back and tripped on a leaf
that now stayed watching its damp edges
in that little forest you stepped into
trying to find cover
from the rain

And, looking around, you let out yet another cry

where are you walking?

Translated by Karen Emmerich

Mladen Lompar

A night in a lapidarium

1

beneath the cypress trees
remnants of carved endearments
with forts and tomb stelae
the baptistery
portal and altar decorations

stones remarkably
huge
but hard for the soul

and there is no time like this
nor another
into which foundations I stare

on one gravestone
(the end of the world and a symbol of senselessness)
a broken name
a stricken messenger
whose message has been abruptly stopped
and the image I discern –
a line
with three uneven stars above
and seven verses of destroyed letters
I sense only the final word
– NIGHT
at the end of seven lines of life
prayer
for accidental believers

for visions and whispers
or silence

2

messages designed for exploration
touching the sunken letters
and gilding of bitterness

your fingers glide
and merge with the petrified endearments
of those who reached nowhere

is this your will
my Lord

what was sinful in those inscriptions
and visions
over the dust
and emptiness

and unfathomable clear purpose

only the words share their power with you
my Lord

but I seek them in vain
and collect the names
of their bones
from fragments of inscribed stone
in this terrible silence
among butterflies and laurel

3

in vanishing light
votive homes
and symbols

eternal silence
inhabited by butterflies
and glow worms

and the sigh of one
not purified
by this horrible godly sin

Translated by Tanja Bakić and Stephen J. Mangan
.

The old Bar

I came across walls
clad in stony suffering
while I walked the deserted streets
as if wandering through a cemetery
long abandoned
and desolate

only the odd well soaked saint or angel
from a wall of the crumbling shrine
appeared for a brief moment
as a gentle silhouette of those
who never truly lived in our eyes

1968

Translated by Tanja Bakić and Stephen J. Mangan

Tanja Bakić

***

In the river I stand
And drink moonlight in my palm
From the frozen bed I pull out a rock –
And cast it high towards the stars.

Goods and chattels of summer.

From myself I go out
And breathe like ice.
From myself I go out
And find out what
Water smells like.
From myself I go out
And realize
The sky lied to me,
That it knew
The secret of the sea.

***

***

The last scent of the garden
And myself captured inside –
The most silent star of all.

The grass calls out to a butterfly.
Bodies rise
And fall in space.

You are becoming a pearl,
The pearl is becoming you.

***

Translated by Peter Stonelake, Stephen J. Mangan and the author

Ekaterina Grigorova

(Normal for Skåne)

I remember the brown water of the Baltic.
The internal discipline of a boundless 16 degrees.
Petra gave an ugly shriek and a flock of ducks shot
into the sky; we shouted wildly, raised our elbows
as if from nettles; our legs kicked
and sank into the seaweed fronds.
Imperceptibly they brought our beautiful housewife
to shore, they plaited her arms like ropes,
they took her to the water
and while summer held to the blown grass,
while the clouds above us departed without hearing,
her face concealed a sigh,
drawn inward and still deeper than a normal thought.

Translated by Tom Phillips

Excursion

Houellebecq at 15 travels with his class.
Germany is a story and he's shoved in his bag
a volume by Pascal.

The column moves in near-inexplicable order:
all anyone sees is the backs of their heads
and they jostle down the Ku'dam.

It happens that the space between them
grows.
Then they gaze at their shoes, crack jokes,
pay no attention to the heavenly girls
as they stumble.

Here they are – people with no chains,
with no death penalty,
who are being killed by love.
Some already are, some will be.
Imagine a line of the unhinged
with exposed arms and legs,
as yet without bodies,
who will love one another,
be free.

Translated by Tom Phillips

Nenad Trajković

A view from two rooms

on your relaxing sofa
I saw some drawings
in which one could stay forever
later a few questions followed
I gave negative answers
in complete negation of everything
I managed for you to disappear

on my relaxing sofa
you saw the drawings with no meaning
after winning the favour
the questions were flowing out of me stereotypically
your no was giving some hope
then you said there was chaos in you
and I did not even exist

like this to a nonexistent shape
you gave the one

Translated by Danijela Trajković

Hours of philosophy

I haven't told you about the world in a way
as we have been taught about it
not as was seen by the eyes of others
everything loses meaning as the time passes
because other people's lies are unsustainable
for a higher level of knowledge
even if we call it the truth
how to explain the notion of axiom essence

you remember your enthusiasm when
I introduced you to the first wise person
you told me the ancient world was not dead
you see I had to notice the majority
who have forgotten Aesop
in this fast and frantic time
forgotten the New Testament
and the quotations used for the foundation
of their wise books

I told you everything spreads
as large as we choose alone
a path from you to me is not of the same length
as the path from me to you
that none of us will ever measure with certainty

so your town is lighter than mine
although we live in the same town
it has nothing to do with my periphery
and your centre
perhaps has more to do with how many times we went out
a daily carnival of masks survives centuries you do not realize it
but I'm going to tell you about one day

you know the day when the company your mother
was working for went bankrupt
you were saying half the better things would be at home
I wanted to tell you that the value of all was fictitious
and watching the tears on your cheek I was pretty sure
weight cannot be determined
but still I only kept long silent beside you
as something appropriate and what was meant

Translated by Danijela Trajković

Vjera Bojanić

To see the path

As if Karuč were bewitched by a dream
Does it hope for flowers and return

It seems to me the Moon has drowned
Pour out the love so I can see the path

Leave me to the stars
So water won't steal them

I'll give myself to the all-seeing lake
That follows me
And I'll give birth to new water from my sky

Translated by Galina Tudyk

The storm

I was thinking
With affections
I could turn
The winter
Into the summer

And I could tame
The water too

Now I'm trembling
By the river
In the storm

And I'm calling
The marble night
To be my sister

Translated by Galina Tudyk

Enes Halilović

The wall of existence

Look!
An earthworm.

It's going somewhere.

I took out a scalpel. I cut it. In two.

In this way from one, two earthworms originated;
and the regeneration started right away.
With time, the earthworms will restore
the half they miss.

I asked two earthworms: when is your birthday?
Then, when the first earthworm was born,
or the day when I cut it in two?

Translated by Danijela Jovanović

A legend of the heroine

That is how the leader of the Chinese Revolution
Mao Zedong was.

He led 86 thousand soldiers
On the Long March.

They overran 12 provinces,
18 mountain chains and 24 rivers.

And won more than three hundred battles.

During the Long March the leader carried
2 blankets, some books, and one table cover made of plastic,
And for 370 days he rode the same mare.

When, in the end, he was asked how she endured,
The leader answered:
*Before the March we hid her foal
So she could still look for him.*

Translated by Danijela Jovanović

Manjola Brahaj

Metamorphosis

My words have risen from the dead and cry sky high
as you fierce Zeus won't pour me into your glass and drink me.

My lips become salty from dusk to dawn over seas of your skin
as you sour Charon won't use me as a map in your boat of shame.

My hands burn in the new moon's fires from clouds down to the earth
as you egoistic Orpheus won't take me in your sound as a note.

My body erodes, melts from the bottom to the highest peak,
as you moonstruck Cheops won't take me to your grave as a bone.

My heart is in pieces and my fate is all tattered
as a love as yours, Adam, I cannot find any more.

Translated by Shqiptar Oseku

To the tree

I've wished so many times to be a tree,
to be like you
in death as in rebirth.

Thousands of seasons have passed your eye,
fingers by thousands caressed your face and body,
but you know to tell:
about the passion of the colours,
about the fierceness of the rain,
about winters' frozen tales.
But you are still there,
and each time I touch you again
I wish to be you,
one with you,
to live the lust of the spring together.

Translated by Shqiptar Oseku

Mitko Gogov

Lobotomy of a lament

Let all cats under the ledges
Speak in their baby talk
Nonsensical nonsense

In the eyes of elders,
Let minimalism be created
By the shadow of the day

– our stolen footballs are forever gutted

Animals do have feelings
But they don't have words to tell us that
A silent echo has burst.

We drown in the sink of imagination
We dream
A bathtub is not one until your
Electric whisper
Falls into it

Yet the century?!

The century crosses the road on a red light
Heavily captured

Enclosed

Frightened as on the face of a doe
With her slow and steady pace
With no joy
Or caress
With no blades of grass
Touching, a trickle forgotten in her eyes

With a country that's twisted and a dance that's stopped
With a noble soul,
Yet desert-like

In chains,
Heavy chains
That ever so slowly
Collapse
Their prattle

Translated by Aleksander Mitovski

Old clothes container

To your hand reaching out for bread
I offer my friendship
On your cardboard – mattress for your dreams,
I draw a house.
I put up lampposts in your life
With wires I connect your dreams and reality.

I change broken street lights
With colourful bright stories
So the holes under your back can forget
Your lips cracked from the cold.

I reflect the smile at the shop window
Which suffers from old plastic dolls,
I give you clothes as a gift together with the toys
From the advert above your head.

In a container I leave your courage
For begging
And
Reward your suffering with
A medal of bravery.

Translated by the author

52

Ranko Pavlović

Hunting

We hunted grasshoppers and butterflies,
Just to have enough play in the meadow...

...then we hunted rabbits and roebucks,
Just to gorge ourselves and to survive,

Then we hunted foxes and wolves,
to stop them hunting our rabbits and roebucks,

then we hunted other hunters,
to stop them hunting our quarry...

...so we started to hunt ourselves,
for he who once starts hunting – never stops.

Translated by Svetlana Pavlović

Abandoned words

Out of crumpled paper
Thrown into the room corner
The words are getting out
Like a fog out of a grove.

They don't want to be abandoned,
They want me to embrace them again,
To give them their dignity back,
They want to be a poem.

If I do not comply with that wish
They sulk and turn their heads,
And when I turn off the lights
They slip into my bed and my sleep.

Washed and smiling,
They wake up in the morning before I do,
And, like white butterflies,
Overfly my desk.

Beamed by their glitter,
I get out of bed drowsily
And hurry to put down again
Last night's abandoned words.

Translated by Svetlana Pavlović

III POETRY FROM MOLDOVA

Ion Buzu

Window blinds

My new job description says I have to write
45 stories of 300 words each,
about window blinds and nothing more, that was the deal,
something there is nothing to write about,
like spitting to get 45 water cups from an empty bucket,
first I had to spit to have some liquid,
45 canfuls of spit.
I am paid 5 farthings per word
John Fante was paid 1 cent per word for prose
and 10 cents for poetry.
I do not write any prose nor poetry,
I write about window blinds, 45 stories,
learning the final lesson of futility,
no one will ever read these texts,
they will only place a website higher on google search,
I'm at the 30th and the bucket is emptied,
my mouth is dry, I take a shot to spit into a cup
and nothing, I grew myself
into a machinery of 3 dollar stories about blinds,
a machinery of the meaningless,
Camus and Cioran would pat me on the back proudly,
I understood the final lesson of futility.
I wrote about blinds used by philosophers,
bamboo for a zen mood,
wood for a state of savagery,
metal for imprisonment;
online poker players use blinds with remote control because they are
                                                        lazy, too lazy
to adjust them by their own hands,
as for the poets, they get drunk, vomit and roar, cursing the heaven
and nobody has any idea because their blinds are always drawn.
I wrote about blinds that get you rid of your depression,
you adjust the right amount of sunlight entering the room
and the depression is healed.
I tried harder to spit into the cup and went on with the writing.
Electric blinds with remote control offer life expectancy to disabled people
because they no longer resort to others to raise them up in the morning

and to get them down at dusk.
I wrote about drivers using blinds for the windows of the car,
office managers have their horizontal blinds to spy on their employees,
thieves are scared in front of a house that has an automatic adjustable
window blinds system,
politicians are safe from snipers because of their adapted blinds,
then I wrote a story about a guy who fell off the chair
and broke his back trying to lift the window blinds by hand,
he would have to buy those by remote control and the calamity
wouldn't have happened.
Beyond the window, Ana was hanging her clothes on the wire, staring
at me interestedly,
watching how I regularly spit into a cup and write after.
I finally ended with the phrase: Blinds are part of our lives.
and pulled down mine.
There's nothing left to see for Ana.

Translated by Cristina Ilie

Grigore Chiper

Wise men reading the stars

You know how to preserve the holiness of a voice
by not talking
or by sharpening the scabbard instead of the dagger
when

The wise men reading the stars
pass by
they prophesy your declaration: give me the strength
to doubt you.

But we shall not unravel the charades of fog
for some time,
not before we squander our childhood
praising life.

In every direction, paths open under my gaze
like flowers.
On these they leave without haste, the magi
who read the stars.

Translated by Sean Cotter

Blue period

You have never been lucky
in games of chance.
You have trudged through books,
but never mastered patience.

Queens with queens, jacks with jacks.
How else? You are only you,
you mix your greens and yellows
on a pallet carved from cashew.

Betting all my colours in a bluff
under the bare calf of a crescent moon,
I painted like Pablo,
when he was blue.

Stay and we will make a toast
reciting along with the Lord. The others?
He will not resurrect that number,
He will overthrow them with slumber.

Translated by Sean Cotter

Arthur Cojocaru

2001: A space odyssey

1999
mom and dad went to bed earlier
was it of concrete or of glass
the plate from Stanley's Kubrick movie?
retarded impotent
made me a retarded impotent
a stanley
made me a black plate
have you made me of concrete or of glass, father?

* * *

"Mother died today.
Or, maybe, yesterday.
I don't know."
– Thanks for coming guys
today Arthur is fauxer then ever
– Sorry guys, but my mom died
I cover my mouth with the scarf

yesterday died daniel's dad
or today maybe,
he doesn't know either
after 3 days daniel's jacket still smells like corpse
my scarf like perfume

Translated by Tatiana Purice

Father's name

My father isn't visiting us anymore
and I can't pronounce his name
my mother does the laundry
in the bathroom
always in the same shirt with the unbuttoned collar
in the middle of the playground
my friends ask me my father's name

I go home, take some soap and help my mother

Translated by Tatiana Purice

Radmila Popovici

the ugly lady

i was ugly in the child´s eyes
it ran
towards its mother for hiding
in her womb there was room
only for dry
bread

i was ugly in the child´s eyes
the crying little girl i was
threw herself into
her father's arms which broke
like two rotten branches
i fell down on my back and
i forgot who I was

i just remembered
that i was ugly in the child´s eyes and
i visited the houses
of all the ugly ladies I kissed them
their rotten nails their wounds their wrinkles
their elbows their heels and I was shouting
as loudly as I could you are
the most beautiful of all

i was ugly in the child´s eyes
and i punished my soul
i kicked on it i slapped it
i blamed it why are you so ugly
you ugly thing the soul looked
down feeling ashamed streams of lyrics
started flowing on his cheeks
lyrics livid because of the feeling pity and spite
i peeled my skin of i put on fire
the hair on my head i pulled
my teeth out one by one i tore
my tongue away then i threw all of them
in the realm of death

i cried deep into my bones
i mourned my betraying flesh my running
blood my mind oh my mind

i gathered all my courage
i took the word "ugly"
in my hands for looking into it
as into
a mirror

i had just gotten old
it was sunny and
quiet

i was ugly in the child´s
eyes

i did not hate it
its eyes were just
inside out

Translated by Mircea Dan Duta

Nicolae Spătaru

the paths will eat anything

little do the kings care that you lead a dog's life
that the mossad
no longer tosses beautiful women your way
it all leaves you baffled:
can you really have sunk so low?
can your grey matter really be devoid
of important secrets?

nowadays nobody lends you a dime
nobody stands you a beer
your erstwhile fans have forgotten you
no more do they ask you to write them stately hymns

your thoughts are now shifting sands
in a desert waste
and your regrets burst
like balloons in the may day parade

you're like the moonstruck traveller
who has scrunched up his paths into balls
next to his varicose legs

from time to time (with a ritualistic gesture)
you tear a strip
of festering skin from your boots
and feed the paths

the paths will eat anything
they're not friendly at all

Translated by Alistair Ian Blyth

you don't know what to reply

the butterflies were running riot
up against your insomnia-misted windowpane

but here comes the bulldozer in sober garb
the mannerly bulldozer
and with astonishing celerity
the conflict is quelled

what else can you do?
you scrape off the grime of the times
until you uncover a metaphor on which
rejoicing you write your body temperature

is that all?
the bulldozer in sober garb asks you
and bewildered
you don't know what to reply

Translated by Alistair Ian Blyth

Moni Stănilă

Let's talk about hunger like we talk about love

1.
A huge knife does not   tell me murder, but   bread. Because I'm hungry.
...
Not famine, not atrocity.

A gentle and sweet hunger, that comes in swiftly at around 2:00 pm
and chews on the gate of my stomach with tiny and soft teeth of
cartilage. Oh, this tiny and playful hunger,

tickles more than it hurts. And it actually behaves,   as it chews
with its jelly teeth the roof of the stomach to the point of gastro-
oesophageal reflux. It comes in the afternoon, for not splitting me
in half, it does not come with despair, but softly   as the
butterflies of a love story. She makes me hers.
...

I say: coq cooked slowly for 3 hours, I say: pizza, pretzel no.
I say not to anything,   cause it's not rape. It's love and
I say mostly   sushi with ginger and wasabi.

2.
Today I eat the way they make love   in cheap American movies,
          with slow   but precise moves
biting just the right way, chewing for a while, lowering eyelids. I feel
the taste of the chilli separated by the silkiness of the mozzarella,
then I feel their tastes mixed together. Like roman legions, the stom-
ach is supposed to bang the shields to each other   ← staccato, equal,
victorious.

Letting the sauce all over my tongue, not swallowing it quickly, as if I
had the mouth full of aspirin.

Not all of the long-term relationships are ideal, but almost all become
functional   if you insist. My little hunger has a functional relationship
with my big craving.   The stomach is a collateral victim   with its
head being banged on the walls. Instead of offering   a sweet and
lying love, my stomach is that cool character   stupidly dying just
to add drama to the film.   The directors don't kill their main
characters; neither does the mouth keep close to specialities
                    based on potatoes.

65

3.
Among the people and   cars parked on the side walk
left right and ahead
            tiring, but   the hand moves and throws from the east to the
            west a plastic bag   with nine pink and round potatoes
            reminding fists of sleeping babies,   the last light beam of
the day spoiling them.
A heart exposed in a thin, transparent bag.   ← shared in joys there is
as many of them as the ways one can cook its nine faces. Starting with
            the simply   boiled   baked   fried
            thing   until stuffing it with mushrooms covered with
            béchamel sauce   ← like someone snuggling under
a clean duvet   when the sun is already up, and one is still
sleeping.

Heart on sight, placed in a plastic bag, after hours, in the city main market.

Translated by Florina Luminos

Alexandru Vakulovski

From *Sights*

(To Benjamin Fondane)

dandelions

under my balcony
all the neighbourhood dogs shit

I can see chicks coming out
from the neighbouring buildings and
are running towards me with
their fat puppies

they shit and run back

even the red bitch with
hidden cubs is
shitting here

it's full of dandelions in the spring

Translated by Florina Luminos

shepherdly

it's spitting
the drops are racing
the yellow leaves

maple walnut linden Indian bean

yellow everywhere

I've reached the age when
it's not enough to be well
only myself

leaves are falling
I drink smoke take
pills for
the faith of the world

Translated by Florina Luminos

IV POETRY & PROSE

Ivan Hristov

From *A Dictionary of Love*

Amber

noun, sing. used as a mass noun only
Fossilized tree resin with a yellow colour;
Related forms: amberlike, ambery, amberous
Amber necklace.
Amber nuggets.
Burning stone
If natural amber is rubbed vigorously
against wool or silk,
it becomes negatively charged.
When Zeus got tired of hearing
the wailing of dead Phaeton's mother and sisters,
he turned them into willows.
Yet they kept weeping.
Their tears fell into the water
like drops of amber,
which the river carried out to the sea

Translated by Angela Rodel

Sapphire

Its name comes from the Greek
sappheirinos – blue
It comes in purplish-blue,
green, yellow, transparent,
orange and pinkish-orange,
it is often used for decorating crowns,
relieving pain,
reconciling contradictions,
giving eternal life to those
who possess it.
Moses received the Ten Commandments
inscribed on sapphire tablets

Translated by Angela Rodel

Katarina Sarić

"100 years with Aleksandra Kollontai"

But I only wanted to protect and defend you
to bury memories of every painful embryo and woe
of social wrong
trenches and weeded roofs
I wanted to prick out your eyes with a golden hook
so you see
to act as your speed bump
that whore at the corner of the street
an orphan a patient a widow
a saint a sinner a boxing bag a spittoon
so you feel better
to drop down to the size of a bean
grey afternoon with no whiff
to be the voice of the first bugle
and that grindstoned sabre
from the hook and the rake
to unbury from the cradle to the grave
each and every sore pestiferous
and to be the first to lie in it by choice
For you I wanted to clench my teeth
to stretch you in the body of a timid runt
and your back to break so I can prove
how much I love you with deeds not platitudes
To break all of your windows and your bogus nails
displays and the windshields
to drag you by your locks onto the waves
of a new revolution
a new word to make up for it
and not be left high and dry
on a ripped off declaration
on consumer basket with flour and oil
on an action sale
on a doormat at the Delta exit
on a bag of soup a sack of grits
To be your Lupa
to mother for you Romulus and Remus
should we build on those forums our world new and brave
so that upstream rushes all that still can breathe

free and out of the groove and forever
against the disgrace of us all
From the handful of ash I would have risen for you
if you could only pardon my extended hand

Translated by Marija Krivokapić

Marija Krivokapić

i breathe glass
it grows from my head
i pluck it to grow faster to grow bigger
and then i chew it, chew chew and gulp
so that i may transmit, reflect, and refract light
i call to my sister sand,
hey sand, sand
sometimes she is deaf but i persist,
sand, you who have been burying and reburying yourself since before
                                                              i was born

sand, i must be as perfect as you
yet those that breathe air are telling stories
they have seen her consume
human footprints
sea waves with those stinking lives
tar too
maybe that's why sand becomes deaf
once i died in sand
desert dogs chased me
desert birds finished me
last i saw was myself in the eye of a black vulture
we live together, me and the eye
till i control light and i kill the eye

Originally written in English

Amela Lukač Zoranić

Last night

I observed you last night,
tired with sad eyes
your face glowed strangely in the dark
illuminating silhouettes on the wall.

Dense air we breathed
drunk with the monoxide
disillusioned by images reflected in our now.

I cried, you smiled,
many books on the shelves
expected the miracle to save us from ourselves,
waited on the right words to be outpoured
from the inside of our horror,
a short *I love you* would save the day
even if it's fake, who would know
just you and I, enough to continue the tragedy.

Originally written in English

Donika Dabishevci

One night stand

I smell your scent
my body trembles lightly
my heart beats slowly
from fear that you will not come
don't make a mistake
because my soul will fragment
and my desperation for you
is stronger than death.

I want to do it
in an endless desert
or an island in the sea
where fantasy flourishes
at its source
in sand and in mud
in water and in sweat
on a starry moonlit night

I want you as I have wanted you
ever like never before
we'll make a kind of love
without words or dreams
just desire

I've never said to you
that you're a stud
and I am seductive
for what else is there in life
nothing remains
touch me
no words
each night without sleep
let's do it

I want to give you the night
like a mother gives to her child
no word
no hostage

no condition
I want to have you
completely naked
to the bone
and to boil
and to melt
to explode
and to be joyful
just because I'm in this world
just because I'm with you
only in this moment
I'll fight to the last breath
I don't want to see you anymore
to feel pain to the bone at separation
to see the coiled noose choke your throat
your gasping breath
your body giving up

No I want nothing to do with you.

Translated by Leni Idrizi

Rosen Karamfilov

Déjà vu

I lost the ability
to cry at funerals
simply because one time
I went to my own

You were there – in January
I looked down and saw
how you lit the next stub
with a match and started to cry

how one of your tears
hit the tip and how
once it was out
it wouldn't relight

then you trod on the stub
threw it left towards the coffin
which unfortunately was empty

Translated by Tom Phillips

Then and there

Winter changes me –
take no notice
forget about the white shifts
deepening in my mind
like the drifts of snow outside

It's cold – but for comfort
I caress you with my right hand
I can caress you with that for an eternity
without my mortal body shaking

some night I will leave it
just like I've left dozens
of rented rooms and exalted chimeras
that's how I'll leave my body too

Translated by Tom Phillips

Jasmina Bolfek-Radovani Mina Ray

'Unbound' Lines: Writing in the Space of the Multilingual

> *I don't think that one can be a bilingual poet. I don't know of*
> *any case in which a man wrote great or even fine poems equally*
> *well in two languages. I think one language must be the one you*
> *express yourself in, in poetry, and you've got to give up the other*
> *for that purpose.*   T. S. Eliot

For a very long time, I could not choose my language of writing. I had Croatian, French and, later, English at my disposal as writing tools; however, choosing one language for me always meant sacrificing my other languages, other cultures, other identities, other parts of Self. I don't want to sound complacent; my experience is by no means exceptional. The question of language choice and/or language loss has been and still is a recurring one for many writers who have either inherited or have come into a prolonged contact with more than one culture/language/identity. Much later, I came to realize that the problem of language choice is a false problem for me as a writer. It would therefore be more true to say that for a very long time I thought I had to choose a language of writing. As, although I was not explicitly forced to think that way, everything around me led me to believe that I had to do so. I felt compelled to choose one language; the monolingual was, and still is, the standard, the norm, the 'default' option.

So, I tried, and tried again to write in one language, and I failed, and failed again; I felt that when I was writing in only one of my languages I was always losing 'something'. That 'something', I came to realize later, is made up not only of notions and concepts, but also of sounds, images, as well as olfactory, emotional, cognitive, pragmatic and kinetic resonances of the words and the worlds I live in. Each of my languages has its own archeology: one of them contains my sensory and sensual memories; the other inhabits my thoughts, my Self, my consciousness; the third has primarily cultural resonances for me that I identify myself strongly with. Only after I decided that I would not or did not have to choose a language, did I arrive at writing, or more precisely, did I arrive at writing poetry.

The process of writing multilingual poetry is for me a poetic and linguistic experiment: a play with language and a language (inter)play. Each of the languages I inhabit has its own timbre, voice, rhythm; it has its own harmonies and melodies, its own colours. Each language mediates my experience(s) of the world differently. This is perhaps why, when I move in a space between languages, I still experience a feeling of loss. At the same time, from this loss, from this lack, comes creativity. It comes in this space of in-between language. This relationship between loss, writing and unwriting is explored in my trilingual poem 'Reveries about language/Sanjarenje o jeziku/Rêveries autour de la langue'.

It might seem surprising that I usually begin by writing a poem in English (a language that I acquired much later than my native and mother tongues, Croatian and French). However, writing in English has become natural for me; it is the language I feel closest to, at one level, and one that I feel most comfortable in inhabiting. At the same time, words in English possess very few emotional resonances for me. To compose poetry in a language that has very little or no emotional resonance for me as a writer may sound paradoxical, yet I have found this lack liberating. My process of writing goes as follows: I first write a poem in English, then I translate it into Croatian and, finally, into French. This process of translation or of a constant moving between languages is an interesting one. Only after translating a poem in English into Croatian, am I able to go back to the English 'original' to perfect it. Through that process of translation, new echoes emerge, rendering the English version more precise, but also enriched with an emotional layer that I feel was lacking there before I moved to translating it into Croatian. With that also comes the realisation that maintaining the concept of the 'original' (language) in the process of translation is an illusion; the concepts of the original and of the translated language become meaningless in the space of the multilingual. Furthermore, the three versions of the poem that I have written become translations of something that does not reside at the level of the linguistic; they become representations, reflections of a non-linguistic form of thought, of a series of images that exist 'before' language and that only acquire their meaning and linguistic form in the system of language. During my writing process, I came to another interesting observation. Contrary to what I expected, my relationship to the French language has become more neutral; sounds, images, words and phrases in French have less emotional resonance for me now (although French is my mother tongue), except for a few images, or words, that somehow retained that status. Such is the status of the French word *écume*, motivated no doubt by my reading of Boris Vian's *L'écume des jours* (1947) that marked me so profoundly. In the English version of the poem, 'Reveries about language', I write:

> My dreams are haunted
> by the emotional resonance of words, images

écume
L'écume se languissant
sur les vagues paraît telle une dentelle

80

fine...

imperceptibly
He stands behind her and touches her naked shoulder
almost imperceptibly

So, while the English word 'imperceptibly' (as the words 'vision' or 'feathers' in the following verses) seems to have an emotional value for me in that language, the French word *écume* has suppressed the English equivalents 'froth' and 'foam' in the poem. The omission of the English equivalents in the poem marks an empty place; it signifies silence. At the same time, the French word *écume* becomes a prime emotional marker in the poem (through it remaining untranslated into English). This process of writing in the space of the multilingual can be further analysed when comparing the three versions of the poem. Through the process of moving between the three languages, words and images in the Croatian and French versions acquire additional emotional resonances and layers of meaning that are present only partially in the English version. At the same time, the three different languages used in the French, and especially in the Croatian version, become traces of each other. They become echoes:

Emocionalna dimenzija riječi, slika

progoni moje

snove

écume
L'écume se languissant
sur les vagues paraît telle une dentelle
fine...
Morska pjena lijeno se odmara, podrhtava
Na valovima
Poput čipke
imperceptibly
He stands behind her and touches her naked shoulder
almost imperceptibly
On stoji iza nje i sasvim lagano dodirne njezino golo rame

Writing poetry in my three languages is for me an experience of identity re-discovery. It is a return to my Croatian (and my Algerian) roots that I thought I had lost through the experience of moving out of the country and (involuntarily) suppressing these parts of my identity. My Croatian has always been in competition with my French; when I arrived in Great Britain, I became much more preoccupied with losing my French than with losing my Croatian. Gradually, Croatian took a more prominent position. Paradoxically, I always viewed French as the language of literature and culture, but I also felt a sense of inadequacy in relation to that language. Consequently, I cannot relate the memory of French to my Algerian roots. Yet, some of my earliest childhood memories go back to summers in Algeria. Until I was five, I visited Algeria during the summer with my family. I remember the intensity of dark red, blue, ochre colours, smells of jasmine and bougainvillea, the garden of orange and lemon trees, my grandmother's cooking outside and my grandfather's driving. The two main languages spoken in that context were French and Algerian. Yet I do not relate these experiences to speaking French. Instead, I still hear echoes, traces of sounds in Arabic. The silent language in my poetry is the Arabic I heard and began to speak as a very young child. It is the language of my Algerian grandparents tattooed on the back of my memory.

Finally, both as a writer and as a researcher, I am fully conscious of the fact that one can fall easily into the trap of nostalgia, something that I have always tried to avoid. All through my adult life I refused to be nostalgic about my Croatian and French/Algerian roots. Reviving the sounds, the images, the smells and the colours of my earlier identities and memories through the kind of poetry I write allows me to tap into parts of my identity that I thought I had lost irrevocably. It is through a much later re-awakening of sensory and sensorial processes of memory recovery that the loss of my Croatian native tongue has become apparent. At the same time, the traces of the Arabic tongue that is part of my Algerian heritage have also resurfaced. These are the parts of Self that I had suppressed, as I was trying not to lose the other equally important part – the French one, whilst also gaining a whole other language – English.

The multilingual poetry I write allows the reader to move between the words and the worlds of my poems. I am conscious of the fact that most readers do not read, speak and understand the three languages I write in, but I hope that they are able to experience the poems in the space of the multilingual as an invitation to embrace the 'unfamiliar' signs on paper through play rather than through fear and uneasiness. This cross-cultural, spatial type of reading may require more openness and concentration, but hopefully it is also one that is more enriching and thought-provoking.

A final word about my multilingual poetry project 'Unbound'. 'Unbound' (which has recently received funding in London from the *Language Acts and Worldmaking* AHRC-funded project) is a new creative project across UK, Croatia, France and Belgium that explores contemporary poetry writing in the context of multilingualism and across different media. It aims to challenge the paradigm of monolingual thinking formed on the premise of one language, one nation and one identity. It brings to the fore the idea of the 'territory' of language as the only possible space to be embraced by any writer working across languages and cultures. It is conceived as a series of evening poetry performances in London, Zagreb, Paris and Brussels presented in Croatian, English and French. These multi-dimensional – sonic, visual and multilingual – 'promenades' or performances aim to show how the spoken word, sound and image can interact in an innovative way to create a series of 'unbound' or free expressions. Ultimately, 'Unbound' aligns itself with the claim in *The White Review* that "poetry is currently the form of writing that is undergoing the most radical regeneration". It aims to bring poetry fully into the twenty-first century by engaging the public in an accessible way that will both surprise and delight but will also be inspiring and thought-provoking.

Notes

'Reveries about language, Sanjarenje o jeziku, Rêveries autour de la langue' by Jasmina Bolfek-Radovani was published in *Still Point Journal* (1, Nov 2015) and more of her multilingual poetry can be read here: https://reveriesofasolitarygazelle.com
'Unbound' is supported by the *Language Acts and Worldmaking* project, the Arts & Cultural Strategy Office, Queen Mary University, London and KIC Zagreb (Cultural Information Centre, Zagreb). Ffi: www.facebook.com/unbound17/
The epigraph comes from an interview with T.S. Eliot in T*he Paris Review* (no.1, 1959).
The White Review can be found at: www.thewhitereview.org
Boris Vian's *L'écume des jours* (Paris: Gallimard, 1947) has been translated into English as: *Froth on the Daydream*, trans. Stanley Chapman (London: Rapp & Carol, 1967); *Mood Indigo*, trans. John Sturrock (NY: Grove Press, 1968); *Foam of the Daze*, trans. Brian Harper (NY/LA: Tam Tam Books, 2012).

Monika Herceg

moustache

in the end the mother said
that he had tried to steal the burst
of overripe fruits before
and surrender as they did to the decay's embrace
with a loop of rope around his neck
after the funeral she didn't leave the attic
for a month and that was dreadfully reassuring
for her and for us
a wet plethora of grief

in every room
I can still sense the whip of silence
stripping our dignity away
inside and outside of us
because there was nothing to talk about

she complains about gout and his fists
somewhere between the ninth and the tenth joint
she still remembers his cracked hands full of blisters
his thick moustache
as on the day he married her

Translated by Jasmina Bolfek-Radovani Mina Ray

birth defects

sometimes women blossom
in the midst of the strongest of blizzards
the story goes it was anka the neighbour
who assisted in the birth of my father
on earthen floor
in front of the fireplace
a thick blanket of snow outside

he was chasing animals as a child
searching in them for
unnoticeable growths of loneliness
like buds that had grown over
inside his throat

he didn't like being among people

when he was five years old
an enraged swarm of hornets
attacked him
from a nest in the hornbeam
he cried for a long time
his eyes swollen from the stinging
then without a flinch
he continued the hide-and-seek game
in tree holes
turning layers of humus over
failing to notice
the change in the width
and the length of his soles
his first moustache
until one day he fell over his own foot
as he would fall over a molehill

Translated by Jasmina Bolfek-Radovani Mina Ray

Goran Milanović

goldmund

they are twitching, they are hanging
by their bare throats flatly facing the night

the occupier thinks death by hanging
is a lesser death, like killing rabbits

or else it would have been easier
with a coin operated guillotine

they are hanging from the balcony
holding empty air in their hands

the thin thread of June
weaves breath after breath for dachau

the massacre of flies
the black painting almost complete

oh no! middle management is sorry
the hanging is interrupted

for technical reasons –
they have run out of rope

merely the banality of good

the banality of banality

hannah arendt

hannah montana

pancakes of emperor penguin eggs

Tulle, 1944

Translated by Jasmina Bolfek-Radovani Mina Ray

tennis of all against all

during a seminar in political philosophy
tom hobbes plays tennis
and says to me –
my boy, without government
there would be no fifth set
without a killer

he hits a deep slice backhand
game of tennis of all against all

it is in the nature of things that every tennis player
fears for his own backhand
every tennis player is a wolf to every tennis player

the state was built on that fear
the fear of the wrongly called
match ball

the bigger the fear the bigger the state
more tennis more killers
more state killers
more state tennis

Translated by Jasmina Bolfek-Radovani Mina Ray

Ndriçim Ademaj

Infusion

The evening's eyes are dripping
as these drops drop inside the infusion bottle
that tightens your wrinkled arm...

tonight I saw the most beloved eyes in the world
as they are sleeping wearily in the bed of this dark hospital
I saw you tired and numbed for the first time
I saw your pain hanging as a pale neon
over the silence of the night...

we have been here several other times
the first time it was when I was born,
you held my name in your wrist,
you were tender then
as an excellent pupil on the first day of school,
you never thought that one day you'd melt down in life
as this boring infusion
that our lives were nothing but two faded autumn leaves...

sirens come and bring other women
other drunk young men killed
in the unwashed streets of Prizren
cars pushing each other
toward the neighbouring hospital graves
you are only sleeping,
you are breathing...

I remember when I used to play with your long hair
and you would tell me short stories
about those who are gone and those who'd come
about father's boredom
and brother's childhood
but about us we never talked
who cares, tonight you'll listen to me long enough
tonight, you won't say anything
about the nights when I would come back home drunk
about time wasted
about women I have loved,
and who never loved me
more than you ever did...

for a long time I've been wanting to find a song for you
but I never had enough time
I was drinking for the one
who left with the very first airplane for the Distant City
where all the sewerage from this world's betrayals is being discharged
for a long time I've been willing to love you like this,
only with my eyes...

it doesn't matter,
what matters now is for you to wake up
see, the light is coming out with some confused raindrops
see, I am here as well,
watching the most beloved eyes in the world
see, you are awakening from a horrible dream
which is leaving like an uncalled taxi
with the last drops of this infusion...

don't give up,
we have all the time in the world to die...

Translated by Fadil Bajraj

Borce Panov

An invisible letter

I would like to write something down
between me and the invisible city
I would like this silent letter
to travel
after the perfect shape of wind
You will ask
How is it possible for a whole city
to be invisible
This is absurd
even for you
You will say
But however, whatever one hawk
just right now
is becoming a wind portrait
which separates the city
on panicky syllables
Moreover, because the hawk is
the roof of one invisible building
where I still live
your poet
who is writing about invisible things
in this city
that is constantly running away from us
and taking away the boundary of our eyes

Translated by Natasha Miladinovic

The mill on an underground stream

that it was a great wisdom to know
how to divert water toward the mill
which would grind the wheat of life.
And for a long time now
the mill of my words has ground
the strange language of wheat
on an underground stream
which no one had wanted to
divert toward their own mill.

Translated by Natasha Miladinovic

Violeta Hristova

Are you a snail or a man
dragging along his soul!?
You want me to be a sea
but you pour me into a glass...
The heavenly furnace shines,
the days have been heated up
and a yearning opens –
bluish as previous ones.
But surely, even
God shall turn back –
to find in your heart
a seed of charity...
What makes you grow up,
if not the sadness?
You have been here for so long,
and you still stumble over the leaves.
I know, even if you crawl,
there is a hidden reason
to drag along your home
towards another past.

But life locked
the door after you...
Are you a snail or a man
dragging along his soul!?

Translated by Milena Milkova

Anđelko Zablaćanski

The destiny of a poet

Night had woken up poets from time immemorial
It opened their souls with the golden key
Then split images from life
So that those would seem small in comparison with a verse

Night had always been dancing a tango of
Thoughts and feelings tides with a poet
In the middle of a boat without a sail and oars
And occupied with turmoil knowledge

Night had always been stealing poets
From reality, the world and themselves
In order to give them power just before sunrise
To live in the verse for years

Translated by Danijela Trajković

On a poet

A poet is not a person who writes verses
But the one who lives them

A poet is not a person who lives verses
But the one who wrestles with a poem

A poet is not a person who wrestles with a poem
But the one who feeds it with his soul

A poet is not a person who feeds a verse with his soul
But the one who spends the night with it

A poet is not a person who does not sleep at night
But the one to whom God gives the word.

Translated by Danijela Trajković

Danijela Trajković

Attention

She had been sliding for years almost every day,
attracting attention to herself,
and no one and nothing but ice could hers
until 1846 when she felt
that the ice was melting below her
when she saw the stranger in front of her,
whose smile was sweeter
than pancakes for Maslenica,
and his power stronger than Yarilo himself.
"I've been waiting for you too long!"
He said in his own language,
"I cannot do it without you anymore. Let's go!"

***

Tonight a Saint Petersburg skate is
sliding down the stone mountain
reaching Orizaba,
which has been hardly breathing
since the nineteenth century,
bringing a fresh, Slavic air with it…
Tomorrow there will be an earthquake in Mexico!

Translated by the author

Notes on Contributors

Ndriçim Ademaj is an Albanian-speaking poet and writer from Kosova whose work has featured in various anthologies and magazines in both Kosova and abroad. It has also been translated into English, French, German and Macedonian. His publications include the poetry collections *Kërkoj diellin* (2008), *Dera* (2010 & 2012) and *Këngë nga Rruga e Farkëtarëve* (2015) and the novel *Pa heronj, pa bujë* (2017). He currently lives in Paris.

Dimitris Athinakis (Drama, Greece, 1981) works as a features editor and cultural journalist for *Kathimerini* daily. He has studied social theology, philosophy and philosophy of science in Athens, Thessaloniki and Amsterdam. He patiently lives in Athens where he has patiently written three poetry collections (*Without us*, 2009; *Short vacation room*, 2012; *Some space for the stranger*, 2016). His poetry appeared in *Austerity Measures* (Penguin, 2016) and in various international journals and anthologies.

Tanja Bakić (1981) is a Montenegrin poet, literary scholar, rock music critic and translator. Her poems have been anthologised in collections such as *World Haiku* (World Haiku Association, 2016), *Capitals* (Bloomsbury, 2016), *Balkan Rose* (PEN Bulgaria & Hermes). She has been a writer-in-residence in several countries and received the 2016 Central European Initiative Fellowship for Writers Award.

Daniel Bănulescu was born in 1960 in Bucharest and is an internationally acclaimed poet, novelist and playwright. He has been awarded The European Poetry Prize by the City of Munster, The Romanian Academy Novel Prize and the Romanian Writers' Association Prizes for Poetry and for Playwriting.

Vjera Bojanić (Podgorica, Montenegro, 1952) has published two books of poetry: *Slutnje i obale/Premonitions and Banks* (1980) and *Daleki dom/A Fareway Home* (1996). Her work has been published in three regional anthologies and numerous journals and newspapers. The president of the Association of Women Podgorica, she has been actively involved in community culture and is a member of several literary organisations.

Jasmina Bolfek-Radovani (pen name: Mina Ray) was born in Zagreb of an Algerian mother and Croatian father. She moved to London in 1995 where she has been living and working ever since. Jasmina started writing multilingual poetry in 2014. Her poetry in English, French and

Croatian has been published in Great Britain, Canada and Croatia. She is the author of a collaborative multilingual poetry project 'Unbound'.

Manjola Brahaj (Tropoja, Albania, 1986) won the Migjeni award for her 2010 debut collection *Calypso's Lament* and was awarded the Rrahman Dedaj prize in Kosovo in 2012. She has published two further poetry collections: *We are not from here* in 2014 and *What is not told doesn't exist* in 2017. Her poems have been translated into Italian, French, Romanian and German.

Anca Bucur is a poet, performance artist, co-founder of frACTalia Edition House and editor at InterRe:ACT magazine. He is one of the most interesting and convincing voices on the Romanian contemporary performative poetry scene.

Ion Buzu was born in 1990 in the village of Ratuş and is a poet and editor, who graduated from the Academy of Economic Studies from Moldova. He writes and publishes in Moldova and Romania.

Magda Cârneci is a poet, essayist, and art historian. A member of the "generation of the 80s" in Romanian literature, she is also one of its leading theoreticians. The former director of the Romanian Cultural Institute in Paris (2007-10), she is currently president of PEN Club Romania and a member of the European Cultural Parliament.

Grigore Chiper, born in 1959 in Copanca, is an essayist, poet, novelist, journalist and translator. His poems have been anthologised, as have his stories and translations. He has received four major awards and is a member of the Writers' Union of Moldova.

Arthur Cojocaru was born in 1999 and is a poet, photographer and creative writing specialist. He is regarded as being one of the most expressive voices among the youngest generations of Moldovan authors.

Donika Dabishevci (1980) is a poet and critic who studied at the universities of Prishtina and Tirana and whose publications include: *Imaging fragile* (2004), *Prose poetry: F. Konica, M. Frashëri, E. Koliqi, M. Camaj, M. Hanxhari* (2015), *I'll come to you as death* (2015) and *La tua robinja* (2017). She is a member of PEN Centre Kosova and the Kosova Writers' Club and is editor of *Gazeta Observer*. Her poems have been translated into several languages.

Caius Dobrescu was born in 1966 in Braşov and is a poet, novelist, journalist, literary critic and analyst. He is the vice-president of the Romanian PEN Club and has been awarded the city of Münster's Prize for European Poetry.

Dinu Flamand was born in 1947 in Prundul Bârgăului and is a poet, translator, diplomat, former Romanian representative to the Organisation Internationale de la Francophonie and a member of the "generation of the 80s". In the late 80s he was granted political asylum in France because of his anti-communist attitudes. He has translated many French, Spanish, Portuguese and Brazilian authors into Romanian (including Pessoa and Neruda).

Mitko Gogov was born in Skopje, Macedonia in 1983. A poet and conceptual artist, his work has been translated into numerous languages around the world and appeared in a wide range of journals and anthologies. His debut collection *Ice Water* was published in 2011. An editor and activist, he also founded and organises 100 Thousand Poets For Change, the international literary festival in Strumica, Macedonia.

Ekaterina Grigorova (1975, Dobrinishte, Bulgaria) is a full-time lecturer in modern Greek studies in the Dept of Mediterranean and Eastern Studies at the New Bulgarian University. Her publications include two volumes of poetry: *Фарадеев кафез/Faraday's Cage* (2013) and *Дъска по мокрия пясък/Board of Wet Sand* (2014).

Erenestina Gjergii Halili is a distinguished political journalist, academic and poet who won the Crystal Pen for Albanian Poetry and an Albanian Excellence award in 2017. Her publications include: *Gjama e erës, Bibliography of Published Albanian Drama* and *Bibulz*. She has participated in national and international literary conferences and is on the editorial boards of several cultural and scientific journals.

Enes Halilović (Novi Pazar, Serbia, 1977) is a storyteller, novelist, poet, playwright and journalist. His most recent publications are: the poetry collection *Zid/The Wall* (2014), the short story collection *Kapilarne pojave/Capillary Actions* (2006), the play *Kemet* (2010) and the novel *Ako dugo gledas u ponor/If You Gaze Long Into An Abyss* (2016). He is the founder of *Sent* and *Eckermann* magazines and his work has been translated into 20 languages.

Monika Herceg was born in Sisak, Croatia in 1990. In 2017, her then unpublished volume *Početne coordinate/Initial Coordinates* won the Goran prize for young poets. The book was published in 2018 and has recently won the Kvirin Award. Her second book won the Na vrh jezika award for the best unpublished poetry volume in 2018, and is scheduled for release in 2019. Her poems have appeared in a number of magazines.

Ivan Hristov is an award-winning Bulgarian poet and literary researcher. His most recent publications include the bilingual collection *American*

Poems (Da, 2012) and his latest poetry book, *Любовен речник/A Dictionary of Love* (Versus, 2018). Since 2010, he has been a member of the organizing committee for the international Sofia: Poetics festival. He currently works at the Institute for Literature at the Bulgarian Academy of Sciences.

Violeta Hristova is the author of nine books of poetry, the most recent of which are *...she said. And came down from heaven* (Ab, 2012), *An Ampoule of Darkness* (2015) and *The Master of the View* (Smisal, 2018). She is the winner of the Georgi Bratonov National Award for Literature, the Maria Belcheva award and other national literary prizes in Bulgaria.

Rosen Karamfilov (1992) is a poet, novelist and journalist from Sofia, Bulgaria. Hs publications include *Орелът и детето/The eagle and the child* (2011), *Стерео тишина/Stereo silence* (2013), *Колене/Knees* (2014), *Церебрална поезия/Cerebral poetry* (2016) and *Въпреки бурите/Despite the storms* (2018). His work has been translated into English, Italian, Hungarian and Turkish etc and in 2018 he received the Sofia: Poetics festival prize.

Roman Kissiov was born in Kazanlak, Bulgaria in 1962. A poet, translator and artist, his work has been translated and published in more than 20 languages and his most recent collections include *The Garden of Secrets* (2014), *Eggs of the phoenix* (2014) and his selected poems *The Mystic Rose* (2016). He has appeared at many leading poetry festivals including the Struga Poetry Evenings and, as a visual artist, has had solo shows in Sofia, Vienna, Berlin and Skopje.

Marija Krivokapić is associate professor of English literature, University of Montenegro, and an internationally published author. Her publications focus on contemporary Anglo-American literature, Native American literature and travel writing. She has edited and co-edited a series of translations of British, Canadian, South African and Native American authors. This is Marija's first poem to be published in English.

Mladen Lompar (1944-2017) was a multi-award-winning poet and art critic and the author of more than 20 poetry collections. He was president of the Montenegrin PEN Centre, the vice-president of the Doclean Academy of Science and Arts, a member of Montenegrin Matica and of the Montenegrin Independent Writers' Association, and the editor-in-chief of the cultural review *Ars*.

Amela Lukač Zoranić is associate professor of English language and literature at the International University of Novi Pazar, Serbia. As a vice-rector for education, she has been closely involved in higher education reform in the region through a variety of international projects. Her research interests focus on Anglo-American literature and culture, critical theory, colonial and postcolonial studies, cultural studies and translation.

Goran Milanović was born in 1983 in Slavonski Brod, Croatia. His poetry has been published in the literary magazines *Poezija*, *Zarez* and *Ajfelov Most*, as well as on the literary portals metafora.hr and strane.ba. He was awarded second prize at the international literary competition Slovo Gorčina for his manuscript *Rudnik stakla/The mine of glass*.

Iulia Militaru is a poet, performer and editor. She is strongly involved in the activity of the frACTalia Publishing House in Bucharest, Blitz Show Revival performing poetry shows and the frACTal Literary Club. She claims her poetry collections are everything but poetry.

Borce Panov (Radovish, Macedonia, 1961) graduated in philology from St Cyril & Methodius University of Skopje and has been a member of the Macedonian Writers' Association since 1998. As well as essays and plays, he has published 10 poetry collections, the most recent of which are: *Vdah* (*The Breath of Life*) (2014), *Human Silences* (2016) and *Uhania* (2017). His work has been translated into English, Ukrainian, Slovenian, Serbian, Bulgarian, Catalonian, Mongolian, Albanian, Romanian and Danish.

Ranko Pavlović (1943) is a poet and short story writer. He has received many awards for his work, which has been translated into Italian, Polish, English, Hungarian, German, Romanian, Dutch and other languages. He lives and works in Banja Luka, Bosnia and Herzegovina.

Ioan Es. Pop was born in 1958 in Vărai and is a poet and member of the "generation of the 80s". He has published numerous poetry volumes in Romania and abroad, is present in many anthologies and has received literary prizes including The Poetry Prize of the Union of the Writers from Romania and The Republic of Moldova, The Niram Art Prize (Madrid), The ASPRO Prize, The Book of the Year (Bucharest) etc.

Radmila Popovici (1972) is a poet and lyricist born in Floritoaia Veche. An exceptional and singular voice on today´s Moldovan poetry scene, her style consists of a unique combination of lyricism and deep intellectual meditation. She is a member of the Writers´ Union of Moldova.

Obren Ristić (1960) is a Serbian poet, short story writer and anthologist. His poems have been published in numerous literary magazines, anthologies and six individual collections, the most recent being *The*

Barbarians of Tomorrow (2015). His work has been translated into several languages and was featured in *Eight Centuries of Serbian Poetry/ Von A bis Z* (2017). He is a member of The Association of Serbian Writers.

Katarina Sarić graduated from the Department of Philosophy and the Department of Montenegrin language and South-Slavic Literature at the University of Montenegro. She has participated in numerous international literary festivals and has published widely in almost all literary genres. Her work includes: the trilogy *Caligat in sole* (2012), the novels *Nađa, uspori! Zgazićeš pticu* (2014) and *Amputirani* (2016), poetry *Gđice teatralne* (2016) and a collection of short stories *Akutna ženska sedmica* (2016).

Carmen Secere (1975) is a poet and a strong female voice from the middle generation of contemporary Romanian poetry. Published in many prestigious Romanian literary reviews, she is a member of several respected literary clubs. She published her debut volume *almost happy* in March 2018 and has already received several literary awards for it.

Nicolae Spătaru is one of the most important contemporary Romanian authors living in Moldova; he is a native of northern Bukovina and his works depict his Brezhnev-era native region, combining irony, sly humour, false naivety and poignant nostalgia. He is the general secretary of the Writers´ Union in Moldova.

Peter Sragher (1960) was born in Bucharest, Romania. He is a poet, translator and photographer and the president of the Bucharest branch of the Romanian Writers' Union Literary Translators. His most recent poetry collections include: the bilingual *ascultă tăcerea vorbind/hear silence speaking* (Lapwing, 2012) and *dimineața sărută genunchiul athenei/the morning kisses athina's knee* (Brumar, 2012). In 2017, he published the prose work *cartea lui david/the book of david* (Brumar, 2017) with watercolours by David-Thomas Sragher.

Moni Stănilă (1978) is one of the most original voices of the younger-middle generation of Romanian authors living in Moldova. Her mostly experimental works crosses the boundaries between poetry, essay and prose. She is much involved in teaching creative writing and thus in the emergence of the next generation of young poets.

Adrian Suciu (1970, Nasaud) is a poet, novelist, the initiator and organizer of cultural programs and of some of the most important Romanian literary clubs and festivals, and the official leader of the Romanian Literary Alternative openly opposing the official Writers'

Union. Widely seen as a future reformer of Romanian literary life, he has been awarded numerous literary prizes.

Danijela Trajković holds an MA in English Language and Literature from the Faculty of Philosophy in Kosovska Mitrovica in Serbia. She is a short story writer, poet, translator and reviewer. Her work has been published by literary magazines, newspapers and anthologies worldwide. Her first book *22 Wagons* was published by Istok Academia, Knjazevac, Serbia in 2018.

Nenad Trajković (1982) was born in Serbia and is a poet, translator, essayist and literary critic. He has published three collections of poetry: *Traces* (2008) *I'll Take You To The Museum* (2011) and *Wind From the Tongue* (2016). His work has been translated into English, Russian, German, French, Polish, Macedonian, Bulgarian and Slovakian. His translations from Macedonian have been published in *Istok* and he is the founding editor of *Pisanija*.

Alexandru Vakulovski (1978) is a poet, prosaist, playwright, screenplay writer, journalist and translator born in Antonești/Suvorov (now Ștefan Vodă). He has published numerous poetry, prose and theatre works and his writing has appeared in many anthologies.

Anđelko Zablaćanski (1959) is a Serbian poet, aphorist and translator who has published seven collections of poetry. He is the founder and editor-in-chief of the online literary journal *Suština poetike* and in 2014 received the St Petersburg Poetry Festival award in Russia.

Andrei Zbîrnea (1986) is a poet, copywriter, journalist, big fan of Borussia Dortmund and maybe the most personal, fresh and expressive voice of the young generation of Romanian poets. He is heavily involved in the Blitz Show Revival poetry project, frACTal Literary Club and a tri-lingual collection with Danish author Claus Ankersen.

Other books by Red Hand Books:

We hope you've enjoyed the latest edition of our newest venture *Balkan Poetry Today 2018* and you might want to take a look at *Balkan Poetry 2017* which started it all.

It was inspired by our poetry magazine *Turkish Poetry Today* bringing the very best of Turkey's remarkable literary past and present to an English reading world.

As well as poetry we also publish fiction, translations, travel and history at Red Hand Books so please go to our website at :

www.redhandbooks.co.uk

to find out more and support independent publishers and booksellers.

Thank you for your support.

Everyone at Red Hand Books

red hand
BOOKS

BALKAN POETRY TODAY 2017

Featuring the work of more than 30 poets from across SE Europe, *Balkan Poetry Today 2017* offers insight into the rich and diverse poetries of a region that has only sporadically emerged onto the literary radar in the English-speaking world. Established writers sit alongside those from the latest generation to add their voices both to the region's poetic traditions and world poetry in general.

This volume also includes an excellent section devoted to contemporary poetry from Bulgaria, an introduction to contemporary poetry from Macedonia and an essay looking at other recent translations of poetry from SE Europe.

~

Balkan Poetry Today is edited by Tom Phillips, a poet, playwright and translator based in Sophia, Bulagaria who has worked closely with writers and artists across SE Europe for much of the last decade and is a published poet in Bulgarian.